Patio Daddy-O
at the grill

Patio Daddy-O

at the grill

great food and drink for your backyard bash

CHRONICLE BOOKS
SAN FRANCISCO

By **GIDEON BOSKER, KAREN BROOKS,** and **TANYA SUPINA**

Copyright © 2008 by Gideon Bosker and Karen Brooks.

Library of Congress Cataloging-in-Publication Data available.

ISBN 978-0-8118-5579-2

Manufactured in China.

Designed by Reed Darmon.

10 9 8 7 6 5 4 3 2 1

Chronicle Books LLC
680 Second Street
San Francisco, California 94107

www.chroniclebooks.com

Dedications

To my mother, Dorka, who always kept my nose to the grill!

—Gideon

To Craig, who can't cook a lick but has all the ingredients of the perfect brother, with love, for always being there.

—Karen

To dear mother, Lydia, who cooks from the heart, and my twin sister, Natasha, who shares my love of food.

—Tanya

CONTENTS

The Grill Is King

It took a decade and a nation's love affair with flames, adventurous food, and unpredictable flavors. But Patio Daddy-O is back at the grill, strutting that ol' fire-dancing prowess along with a more sophisticated attitude and some new ideas about a culinary form that has never enjoyed more notoriety or respect.

The rudimentary formula of fire, fork, and foodstuff has not changed since Homer's epic heroes in *The Iliad,* with five-pronged spits in hand, put meat "upon the spits, roasted them till they were done, and drew them off." Grilling, then and now, is the pre-eminent brand of public cuisine, an occasion for bare bones displays of culinary mastery, where hosts and guests come together in one long, blissful, lip-buzzing encounter.

It still takes the same PLC (prep, light, cook) to grill ribs as to barbecue them. As any aficionado knows, grilling itself is still sacramental, with its hovering over the flames, prodding, poking, flipping, jabbing, probing, and piercing. What is different is a willingness, a demand even, to think beyond the basics, to grill with some complexity, wit, and worldly influences.

This isn't a Grilling 101 book. Nor is it simply a take on the daddy-dominated patio bashes of the 1950s—the bones of our original *Patio Daddy-O* cookbook. This Patio Daddy-O has gone global, mixing old-school ribs, steaks, and burgers with cross-cultural spice rubs and culinary mash-ups in a new collection of recipes rooted in soulful Americana, yet totally different.

So come join us and discover a few new backyard moves, including hot-off-the-coals corn rolled in Parmesan, butter, and basil (page 71) and a collection of rubs and marinades that mingle garlic, grassy herbs, exotic spices, limes, and other fire-breathing potions (pages 16 to 29). Our recipes presuppose easy access to the kinds of foods found in cities with ethnic neighborhoods. We pitch our counterpoint of flavors to taste buds open to adventure. You can expect to find playful ideas (say hello to our grill-heated S'mores Cake on page 88) as well as unholy alliances, including wicked pork ribs with their own Mexican-Chinese–Deep Southern juju (page 50).

In short, the instructions will be familiar, but the building blocks are new.

Our "heat me, eat me" recipes are designed to bring out the sheer animal charisma at the heart of the grill experience, but without succumbing to the mega-BTU school of grilling. We won't tell you to run out and buy a three-car-garage sized muscle rig with enough BTUs to accelerate global warming. We're savvy about the fact that, no matter what the size or shape of the tool you bring to the job, it's

grilling that makes the man, and if it ain't grillin', it's frillin'!

But first, a caveat: Grilling is not about satisfying the primary need for food. It's all about a guy's secondary needs: for marking turf, consolidating power, showing off, and staging the timeless host-guest rituals at the base of community. What is the backyard invitation if not a kind of manly theater, both rehearsed and improvised, a showcase for imagination, ingenuity, and disposable income?

Any guy can produce a good dish off the grill by following the rough guides of time and temperature a standard recipe will give. But that's only the start. True success is a kind of arcane, secret knowledge passed by word of mouth or learned by patient watching, tasting, and listening. Even decoding the sounds of Man at the Grill—the humming, sighing, wheezing, and twittering—takes the kind of self-mastery that goes into the making of saints and heroes.

Which is why grilling is the only culinary genre that comes with a patron saint attached. The blessed personage in question is Alexander of Comana, dubbed "the Charcoal Burner," a guy who manufactured the stuff until he was elevated to the calling of bishop, a post Alexander served until he was released from his "mortal coil" through martyrdom by fire in the third century. Saint Alexander's feast day is celebrated on August 11, at the very height of the outdoor grilling season.

Digressions aside, our formulas are designed to help max out the "oooh" reflex on every front, from performance to ingestion, and to bring it within reach of a demographic that has been left out in the cold for too long. We're talking city dudes—urban, cosmopolitan, culturally diverse barbecue wannabes who pore over Weber Grill catalogues and dream of reproducing the pyrotechnics of the suburbs within the stringent specs of a fire escape or rooftop terrace.

Meaning: You'll need nothing more than a safe container, fire, and a grate to succeed with our recipes. You may want to jump on the baroque grill bandwagon and get yourself one of those pimped-up cooking machines that do everything but slaughter the cow. But that's not essential. Our instructions will work on any one of five basic grill types: the barrel, brazier, cart, hibachi, or kettle. Take your pick.

Ultimately, as you transfer the goods from grate to platter, we hope you'll discover what makes fire-pit cuisine so potent: Nothing else so vividly awakens the dormant memories of our primordial nomadic ways as when the gang draws close around the flames and turns its back on danger to cook, eat, and tell stories of hardships overcome, rivals disarmed, and death, if only for the moment, evaded.

Yes, grilling is theater—of the most dramatic kind.

But enough philosophizing. Bring on the grub, turn up the heat, and slap the meat to the metal. And, above all, remember: If it ain't grillin', it ain't thrillin'!

—Gideon Bosker, Karen Brooks,
and Tanya Supina

Grilling Like a Pro
Tips and tricks to get you through the tough times

At heart, every guy is a pyromaniac, and the outdoor pit is where you get away with it. What you can't get away with is performance anxiety. The following guide should turn a backyard bash into a triumph of the grill.

Quest for firepower: The type of grill you use is unimportant. Anything that holds enough lump charcoal or briquettes and has a grate will do the job. Don't get hung up on designer grills. A grill is just a grill.

Mesquite rules: Serious fire-pitters know that mesquite lump charcoal provides the most even heat. For convenience, you might prefer standard briquettes, regular lump charcoal, or hardwoods. What makes mesquite charcoal special is that it burns hotter than any other fuel—up to 200 to 400 degrees hotter—so it cooks more quickly. But note: Mesquite takes longer to heat up to the coal stage. You'll want to stand back after you light it, as this fuel likes to spit and pop.

Where there's smoke there's flavor: To impart a savory, smoky taste to meat, poultry, or fish, use a combination of hardwoods (described below) and charcoal. Add a few untreated wood chips—soaked in water for at least 30 minutes—directly to the coals 5 to 10 minutes before you start grilling. For more intense smokiness, add larger untreated wood chunks, soaked in water for at least 1 hour.

Learn to love your wood chips: Hickory wood chips are most common, but you can also tap into maple, apple, oak, mesquite, or cherry. Ideally, the wood should be aged for at least 1 year, so cutting a limb off the neighbor's maple tree prior to party time is not advisable. Moreover, not all hardwoods are good for cooking. Avoid cedar, spruce, pine, and all other resinous options. Once you've picked your wood, remember that it needs to burn down to an ashy ember before it's ready for cooking.

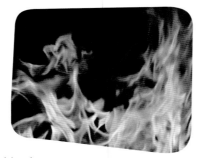

Smoke Signals
How to judge the heat of the fire

Cooking a slab of meat requires a hotter fire than a vegetable kebab does; the key is learning how to gauge the temperature of your coals. (For gas grills, preheat the ceramic briquettes to the desired temperature for about 15 minutes.)

Hot fire: You'll see a red glow through the ash coating.

Medium-hot fire: A faint red glow and a thick coat of gray ash.

Low fire: Almost no red glow and a preponderance of gray ash.

The fail-safe hand-check method: Hold the palm of your hand, face down, about 5 inches above the grate. Count off the seconds until you have to pull it away: 2 seconds for a hot fire; 3 to 4 seconds for a medium-hot fire; 5 or 6 seconds for low heat.

Lose the lighter fluid: In short, avoid if possible. Soaked briquettes can impart an unpleasant taste to grilled foods. Also pass on presoaked coals, which contain the same chemicals as lighter fluid. A charcoal chimney is a handy device that bypasses the nasty stuff (see below).

How to light your fire: As previously mentioned, we avoid lighter fluid—for environmental as well as aesthetic reasons. If you live in a state

where such starters are still legal, be careful. It's all fun and games until somebody becomes the main course. Ouch!

A more sensible alternative is good old-fashioned newspaper kindling. Twist a couple of newspaper sheets up tightly and put them on the bottom of the grill, add some charcoal, and simply light the paper. If this is just too Boy Scout for you, consider the electric charcoal starter wand, a heating element that sits under a heap of charcoal; plug it in and voilà—you don't even need matches. Most grillers prefer a chimney starter, a can-shaped metal container with two compartments. You put crumpled newspaper in the bottom and the charcoal on top, and light the paper. Once the coals have stopped flaming, dump them into the grill. If you're still not happy with these choices, check the Internet for ready-to-light briquettes that claim to flame in 3 to 5 minutes and are only slightly more expensive than standard charcoal.

Baby, it's coals outside: Timing is everything in the grilling world. Don't even think about starting to cook until the coals are coated with a thin layer of gray ash. There's nothing worse than having your guests stand around while your coals are heating up. Give yourself enough time to get the coals ready. Generally speaking, 30 minutes is about right.

How will you know when the time is right? It depends on how quickly you want your food to cook. The more visual the red glow—in other words, the hotter the coals—the quicker the cooking time. Waiting for the coals to heat up can be a great social time. Put on the music, greet the guests, pour the cocktails.

Extinguish the coals: When you're done cooking, douse the coals with water or place the cover on the grill and close the vents. Coals left unextinguished can continue to glow for days—underneath the ash, invisible to the naked eye—just waiting to burn curious little hands.

If you go the gas route: Die-hard aficionados frown on gas grills. Grilling is supposed to take you back to a better, more natural world, and propane is not part of that journey. But if that's not your bag, you'll be ready to cook in about 15 minutes: no survival maneuvers, no fuss, no muss. Your biggest decision will be whether to turn the knob to medium, high, or low. To fire up the grill, consult the manufacturer's instructions. Make sure your cooking rack is clean and preheated before placing food on it.

How to add sass with gas: The traditional smoky flavor produced by charcoal is sacrificed for the sake of convenience with gas grills, but you can compensate. Placing wood chips or charcoal directly on gas burners or lava rocks is not recommended, so try this: Soak some untreated hardwood chips in water, then place in a disposable aluminum pan. Poke a few holes in the bottom of the pan and set on the lava rocks. The wood chips will preheat along with the grill, and they'll start smoking as you cook. (No disposable aluminum pan? Wrap the wood chips in a foil packet and poke holes in the top so the smoke can escape as you cook.) Luckily for you, many wood-chip products at your corner grocery store include an aluminum container inside the package. Another alternative: a "liquid smoke" product, added to a marinade or sauce, can produce the same effect as actual smoke.

Be a Mr. Clean: A clean, lean rack, scrubbed with a stiff wire brush and lightly oiled, is essential to prevent food from sticking or picking up icky remembrances of things repast. This task is most easily accomplished when the rack is hot, and the wise guy attends to this as soon as the grill-fest is complete.

CHAPTER 1

The Rub Club

Rubs, pastes, and other deep treatments for members and guests, plus a couple of handy condiments to help you join in the fun

Mucho Macho Roasted Garlic Rub

Demonic Flavor Booster

Twelve Flavors Fez Blend

Fire + Salt Caramel-Fennel Rub

Peach and Sweet Onion Jamba

Salsa of the Damned

Self-Defense Asian Marinade

The Best Beer Brine

Mucho Macho

Is there anything sadder than barbecue ennui? That's where this mood booster comes in. Blending macho Mexican swagger with the tingle of Caribbean spices, it's deep, complex, and not for the timid— perfect for those days when you're staring into the belly of your grill and can't conjure up anything more inspired than ribs and red sauce. If you're really flying, try grapefruit juice rather than the orange. Zowie.

Roasted Garlic Rub

8 medium cloves garlic, peeled

1 tablespoon each: salt and ground cumin

1 teaspoon ground cloves

$1/2$ teaspoon ground allspice

2 tablespoons coarsely chopped hot chile (jalapeño, serrano, or arbol)

$1/4$ cup fresh cilantro leaves

$1/3$ cup orange or grapefruit juice

1 teaspoon fresh lime juice

3 tablespoons olive oil

⟶ The rub will keep for up to 6 days, covered and refrigerated, but it is best used immediately.

1. Roast the garlic cloves in a dry skillet over low heat until lightly browned, about 7 minutes.

2. In a food processor, combine the salt, cumin, cloves, allspice, chile, cilantro, and roasted garlic. Add the citrus juices and olive oil and process to a paste. Coat the food to be grilled and marinate, refrigerated, until ready to grill.

Marinating times: whole chicken, 3 to 4 hours; chicken breasts and thighs, 2 to 3 hours; fish fillets or shrimp, 1 to 2 hours; steaks, 2 to 3 hours.

Makes about 1 cup

Demonic Flavor Booster

This is the Christopher Walken of barbecue pastes— a little cracked and off-kilter, with the ability to lift everything around it. Thick with smoky ancho chile heat, sweet vinegar tang, and the bright pungency of cilantro, it's a pure pop of decisive flavor with a versatile profile. Use as a marinade for chicken or beef, swab over burgers as a condiment, or dab in pasta salads in need of liftoff.

4 dried ancho chiles, stemmed and seeded

4 cloves garlic, chopped

3/4 cup coarsely chopped fresh cilantro

1/3 cup olive oil

2 teaspoons chopped peeled fresh ginger

2 teaspoons soy sauce

2 teaspoons balsamic vinegar

1 teaspoon each: ground cumin, brown sugar, kosher salt, and ground black pepper

1. Soak the chiles in hot water until soft (30 minutes to 1 hour). Drain and transfer to a food processor. Add the remaining ingredients and purée until smooth. Coat the food to be grilled and marinate, refrigerated, until ready to grill.

⟶ This will keep for up to 3 weeks, topped with a thin layer of olive oil, covered, and refrigerated.

Marinating times: steaks, 30 minutes to 3 hours; whole chicken, 2 to 4 hours; chicken breasts and thighs, 2 to 3 hours; vegetables, 30 to 60 minutes; fish or shrimp, 1 to 2 hours.

Makes about 1 cup

LE RÉVÉLATEUR DES ATHLÈTES

Twelve Flavors Fez Blend

At last, a paste to rock the casbah—or at least your backyard. The flavors evoke Morocco's mazelike souk itself, hidden and rambling, mysterious and sensory. While North Africa is the inspiration, the final production twists and turns on spikes of fresh lime.

4 large cloves garlic

1/4 cup fresh lime juice

1 1/2 tablespoons sweet paprika (preferably Hungarian)

1 tablespoon honey or brown sugar

1 tablespoon kosher salt

1/2 teaspoon each: ground ginger, cardamom, cumin, cloves, cinnamon, allspice, and cayenne pepper

5 tablespoons olive oil

1. In a food processor, combine all of the ingredients, and process to a paste. Coat the food to be grilled and marinate, refrigerated, until ready to grill.

⟶ This will keep for 1 month, covered and refrigerated, but it is best used immediately.

Marinating times: whole chicken, 3 to 4 hours; chicken breasts and thighs, 2 hours; fish fillets or shrimp, 2 hours; lamb chops or leg of lamb, 2 to 4 hours.

Makes about 1 cup

Fire + Salt Caramel-Fennel Rub

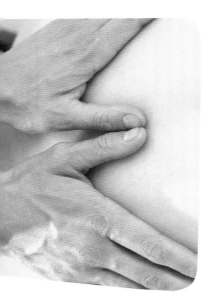

Let's face it: Meats destined for the grill need more pampering than Madonna. A backrub of spices and aromas can charge up flavors and buff the surfaces, encouraging a crackling chew when seared. Here, the licorice perfume of fennel is unleashed with pepper zing, salt, and lemon zest (the yellow-only part of the rind that you remove with a peeler)—plus just enough brown sugar to elicit sensuous caramel undertones. Ay, there's the rubdown.

2 tablespoons ground fennel seeds

1 tablespoon red pepper flakes

2 tablespoons chopped lemon zest

1 tablespoon light brown sugar

3 tablespoons salt

1. Combine all of the ingredients in a small bowl. Stir well to blend. Coat the food to be grilled and marinate, refrigerated, until ready to grill.

——➤ The rub will keep for 5 weeks, covered and refrigerated, but it is best used immediately.

Marinating times: whole chicken, 3 to 4 hours; chicken breasts and thighs, 1 hour; fish fillets or shrimp, 2 to 3 hours.

Makes about 1/2 cup

Peach and Sweet Onion Jamba

Summer provides endless opportunities to chew the right thing. And when peaches are calling, this condiment is the move to make. Sweet on first meeting, but with a backbeat of spicy rhythms, it can transform a simple grill into something that makes you want to dance on the tabletops. So what if your cooking skills bring to mind Kevin Federline doing opera? If you can chop, you can make this— in a hip-swirling flash.

3 large, ripe peaches, peeled, pitted, and diced (about 2 cups)

3 tablespoons minced sweet onion or green onions (white part only)

3 tablespoons chopped fresh basil

Pinch of cayenne pepper, or hot pepper sauce to taste

2 tablespoons olive oil

1. In a medium bowl, combine all of the ingredients. Enjoy immediately, or cover and refrigerate for up to 2 weeks.

⟶ Best served with: grilled swordfish, halibut, sea bass, shrimp, pork loin, or chicken.

Makes 2 1/2 cups

Salsa of the Damned

You'd have to be possessed to combine pineapple, mint, and red onion with enough naked intensity to fuel a party gone mad. We don't recommend this sweet, cool, and sharp condiment to everyone—only people who like to eat like crazy.

1 small to medium pineapple, peeled, cored, and diced

3/4 cup minced red onion

6 tablespoons chopped fresh mint

1 tablespoon fresh lemon juice

1/2 teaspoon cayenne pepper

1 teaspoon salt

3 tablespoons olive oil

1. In a medium bowl, combine the pineapple, onion, mint, lemon juice, cayenne, and salt. Stir, cover, and chill for about 1 hour so the flavors can blend.

2. Just before serving, drain the salsa and add the olive oil. Use immediately, or cover and refrigerate for up to 2 weeks.

——→ Best served with: grilled shrimp, fish, chicken, or pork.

Makes 4 to 5 cups

Self-Defense Asian Marinade

The savvy Patio Daddy-O needs at least one Asian marinade with more kicks than Bruce Lee. This one arrives with a quick burst of sweet, salty, and spicy flavors, then slyly moves to a shadowy crush of aromatics. As Lee would say (while crushing a shin), "Hii-yaahh!"

1 tablespoon each: ground coriander, Chinese five-spice powder, and ground fennel seeds

2 tablespoons each: minced garlic and minced shallot

1 tablespoon grated peeled fresh ginger

2 tablespoons honey or brown sugar

1 teaspoon hot chili powder, chile paste, or chili flakes

1/3 cup each: fresh lemon juice, soy sauce, and olive oil

1. Combine all of the ingredients in a small bowl, and stir well to blend. Pour over the food to be grilled and marinate until ready to grill.

Marinating times: whole chicken, 3 to 4 hours; chicken breasts and thighs, up to 1 hour; fish fillets or shrimp, 1 to 2 hours; country-style boneless ribs, 2 to 4 hours; duck breasts, 2 to 4 hours.

Makes about 1 1/2 cups

⟶ The marinade will keep for 2 weeks, covered and refrigerated.

The Best Beer Brine

Why is one person's chicken dry as hell's waiting room while another's is impossibly moist, like something straight from the dining room of paradise? Some would say the answer is simple: food + brine + searing = heaven. Typically, a brine is a marinade of salt, sugar, and water, a combination that creates the right chemistry to seal in succulence. Score an A on your lab test with the addition of beer—the bubbles seem to penetrate surfaces, adding their own surge of moist intensity. Sure, a brine is extracurricular work, but the results separate the students from the teachers.

1/2 cup firmly packed brown sugar

1/2 cup kosher salt

1 cup hot water

1 tablespoon chopped lemon zest

2 teaspoons chopped fresh thyme

2 teaspoons chopped fresh rosemary

3 bay leaves

2 teaspoons black peppercorns, crushed

7 juniper berries, crushed

Two 12-ounce bottles cold beer (medium body)

1. In a large bowl, combine the brown sugar, salt, and hot water, and stir until dissolved. Add the lemon zest, thyme, rosemary, bay leaves, peppercorns, juniper berries, and beer. Stir well to remove the carbonation. Place the meat in the bowl with the brine and refrigerate. Add cold water, if needed, to cover the meat.

Brining times: pork, 4 to 6 hours; whole chicken, 4 to 5 hours; chicken breasts and thighs, 2 to 3 hours; tuna, 3 to 5 hours.

Makes about 4 1/2 cups

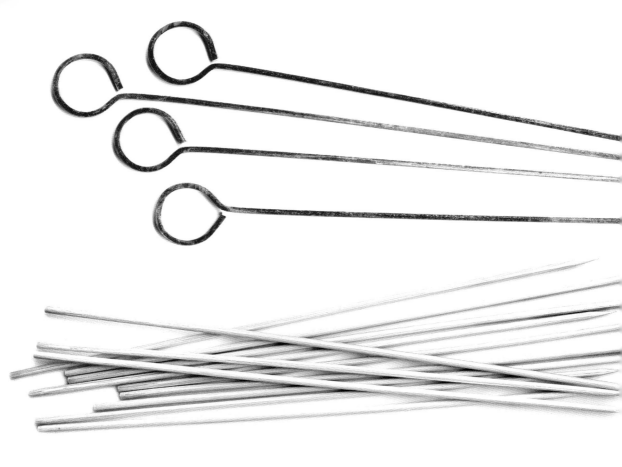

CHAPTER 2

Sword swallowing for fun and flavor

Love That Kebab

Bollywood Chicken 'Bobs

With its plinky wail of cumin and cardamom, this tandoori-style Indian marinade can transform chicken into something special: part spicy, part tart, all tender. Contributing to the effect is the yogurt itself—the density helps hold spices to the surface while the blast of creamy acid helps break down any resistance from the meat. Consider this the perfect way to levitate your karma, in case you were no more than a teriyaki stick in your past life.

Marinade

1 cup plain yogurt, preferably whole milk

2 cloves garlic, minced

1 jalapeño chile, seeded and minced

1 tablespoon ground cumin

2 tablespoons chopped fresh cilantro

3 tablespoons fresh lime juice

1 tablespoon minced peeled fresh ginger

2 tablespoons olive oil

1/2 teaspoon ground cardamom

1 teaspoon salt

2 pounds boneless, skinless chicken breasts, cut into 2-inch cubes

2 red onions, cut into wedges

1 pint cherry tomatoes

Vegetable oil for the grill

1. In a large glass bowl, combine the marinade ingredients. Add the chicken and marinate in a cool place for 30 to 45 minutes.

2. Soak eight 10- to 12-inch bamboo skewers in water for at least 30 minutes. Prepare a medium-hot fire in a charcoal grill, or preheat a gas or electric grill to medium-high.

3. Using a slotted spoon, remove the chicken from the marinade; reserve the marinade for basting. Thread the chicken, onions, and tomatoes alternately onto each of the skewers.

4. Brush the grill grate with vegetable oil. Grill the kebabs until the chicken is done, 7 to 10 minutes on each side, basting occasionally.

Serves 4

Tequila King Shrimp Kebabs

Few things in life are as sweet as tucking into a skewer of charred shrimp and red peppers threaded with hot wedges of juice-squirting limes. The whole production is pre-soaked in a sweet-hot tequila marinade zipped with garlic and cilantro and more of that sassy citrus. One bite and, as a mariachi would sing, "Though I do not want to, I am going to die of love!"

Marinade

2 ounces (1/4 cup) tequila

2 tablespoons fresh lime juice

2 cloves garlic, minced

1 jalapeño chile, seeded and minced

2 teaspoons brown sugar

1/2 teaspoon salt

2 tablespoons chopped fresh cilantro

2 tablespoons olive oil

11/2 pounds large, fresh shrimp, peeled, tails intact

1 red bell pepper, seeded and cut into 1-inch pieces

2 limes, cut into 1/2 -inch wedges

Vegetable oil for the grill

1. In a large glass bowl, combine the marinade ingredients. Stir in the shrimp. Cover and marinate in a cool place for 20 to 30 minutes.

2. Soak eight 10- to 12-inch bamboo skewers in water for at least 30 minutes. Prepare a medium-hot fire in a charcoal grill, or preheat a gas or electric grill to medium-high.

3. Using a slotted spoon, remove the shrimp from the marinade; reserve the marinade for basting. Thread the shrimp, bell pepper, and lime wedges alternately onto each of the skewers.

4. Brush the grill grate with vegetable oil. Grill the kebabs until the shrimp are opaque, about 5 to 6 minutes on each side, basting occasionally.

Serves 4

Pineapple-Duck Sticks with Dark Rum Glaze

These rosy chunks of duck and pineapple are splashed with enough buttery rum to make Captain Jack Sparrow's mascara run. May we suggest a side of rice cooked in coconut milk instead of water, not to mention a round of X-treme Dark 'n' Stormies (page 81). Hoist your forks, mateys.

Marinade

$1/2$ cup soy sauce

$1/4$ cup fresh lemon juice

$1/4$ cup balsamic vinegar

2 tablespoons honey

3 cloves garlic, chopped

1 tablespoon chopped fresh thyme

1 tablespoon chopped fresh rosemary

2 tablespoons grated peeled fresh ginger

Ground black pepper to taste

$11/2$ pounds boneless duck breast, skin left on, cut into 2-inch cubes

Rum Glaze

1 tablespoon unsalted butter

2 tablespoons dark brown sugar

2 ounces ($1/4$ cup) dark rum

$1/2$ ripe pineapple, peeled, cored, and cut into 2-inch cubes

Vegetable oil for the grill

1. In a medium glass bowl, combine the marinade ingredients. Add the duck and marinate for 1 to 2 hours in the fridge. Bring to room temperature before grilling.

2. To make the glaze: Melt the butter in a small saucepan over low heat. Add the brown sugar and rum and cook, stirring frequently, until the sugar is dissolved, 2 to 3 minutes. The glaze should get syrupy; watch carefully to prevent burning. Cover and keep at room temperature.

3. Soak eight 10- to 12-inch bamboo skewers in water for at least 30 minutes. Prepare a medium-hot fire in a charcoal grill, or preheat a gas or electric grill to medium-high.

4. Using a slotted spoon, remove the duck from the marinade; discard the marinade. Thread the meat and pineapple alternately onto each of the skewers.

5. Brush the grill grate with vegetable oil. Grill the kebabs for 3 to 5 minutes on each side for medium-rare, or 7 to 10 minutes to cook the duck through. Brush with the glaze at least once on each side.

Serves 4

Red Army Beef Kebabs

Armed with sirloin chunks and near-lethal amounts of onions and parsley, this fallen-away recipe for shashlik returns a Ruskie classic to its euphoric glory. Follow your marching orders: Marinate for 6 hours, thread, grill to medium-rare, and baste frequently to keep up the juicy morale. Eaters of the world unite—for the Kebab Party.

Marinade

3/4 cup white wine vinegar

3/4 cup red wine

1/3 cup olive oil

5 cloves garlic, chopped

4 bay leaves

1 cup chopped fresh parsley

1 large yellow onion, thinly sliced

1 tablespoon brown sugar

3 tablespoons salt

1 tablespoon ground black pepper

1 1/2 pounds top sirloin, cut into 2-inch cubes

12 small fresh mushrooms

2 red onions, cut into wedges

Vegetable oil for the grill

1. In a large glass bowl, combine the marinade ingredients. Add the beef. Cover and refrigerate for at least 6 hours or overnight.

2. Soak eight 10- to 12-inch bamboo skewers in water for at least 30 minutes. Prepare a medium-hot fire in a charcoal grill, or preheat a gas or electric grill to medium-high.

3. Using a slotted spoon, remove the meat from the marinade; reserve the marinade for basting. Thread the meat, mushrooms, and onions alternately onto each of the skewers.

4. Brush the grill grate with vegetable oil. For medium-rare kebabs, grill 3 to 4 minutes on each side, basting occasionally.

Serves 4

Party Animals Apricot and Pork Skewers

Are you experiencing trembling and twitching or white-knuckled, heart-pounding terror? Oh, you're having a party! Don't sweat it, man. All you need is one killer recipe (this one has its own special spicy-sweet Asian-oompah gestalt) and one run to a Chinese grocery store to stock up on cool, inexpensive Asian crackers and nuts. Stock a cooler with fun beers and sodas, then activate the cooking plan by marinating the pork the night before.

Marinade

3 cloves garlic, minced

5 tablespoons soy sauce

3 tablespoons sherry vinegar

1 tablespoon brown sugar

1 tablespoon fresh lemon juice

2 tablespoons ginger preserves

2 teaspoons Thai or Vietnamese
   chile paste

1/4 cup olive oil

1 1/2 pounds pork tenderloin

6 firm, ripe apricots, pitted and
   quartered

Vegetable oil for the grill

1. Combine the marinade ingredients in a large glass bowl.

2. Cut the tenderloin in half lengthwise, then cut crosswise into 1 1/2 -inch-long pieces. Add the pork to the marinade, stirring to coat the pieces. Cover and refrigerate for 30 minutes to 3 hours.

3. Soak eight 10- to 12-inch bamboo skewers in water for at least 30 minutes. Prepare a medium-hot fire in a charcoal grill, or preheat a gas or electric grill to medium-high.

4. Using a slotted spoon, remove the pork from the marinade; reserve the marinade for basting. Thread the pork and apricots alternately onto each of the skewers.

5. Brush the grill grate with vegetable oil. Grill the kebabs until the pork is done, 12 to 15 minutes, turning and basting frequently. Serve at once.

Serves 4

Voodoo Fruit and Fish Fingers

What happens when hunks of fish soak up a potion of sweet, sour, gingery, mustardy juices and then sizzle on skewers alongside the sweet pop of fresh peaches? A dish that's just scary good. This is eating as pure desire—and it's bound to put a spell on you.

Marinade

$2/3$ cup fresh lime juice (5 to 6 limes)

$2/3$ cup olive oil

$2/3$ cup dry white wine

5 tablespoons chopped fresh cilantro

3 tablespoons soy sauce

3 tablespoons honey

4 cloves garlic, minced

$1^1/2$ tablespoons grated peeled fresh ginger

1 tablespoon Dijon mustard

$1^1/2$ pounds swordfish, cut into $1^1/2$-inch cubes

1 pint cherry tomatoes

2 large peaches, pitted and each cut into 8 slices

16 large green onions (white part only), about 2 inches long

Vegetable oil for the grill

1. Combine the marinade ingredients in a large glass bowl. Add the swordfish. Cover and marinate for 30 to 45 minutes in a cool place.

2. Soak eight 10- to 12-inch bamboo skewers in water for at least 30 minutes. Prepare a medium-hot fire in a charcoal grill, or preheat a gas or electric grill to medium-high.

3. Using a slotted spoon, remove the fish from the marinade; reserve the marinade for basting. Thread the fish, tomatoes, peaches, and onions alternately onto each of the skewers.

4. Brush the grill grate with vegetable oil. Grill the kebabs until the fish is cooked through, about 5 minutes on each side, basting occasionally. Serve at once.

Serves 4

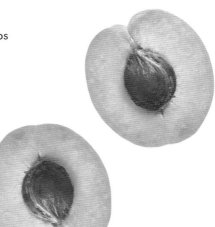

Mighty Mint-Scented Lamb Kebabs

Knobs of lamb and vegetables threaded on rosemary branches have become a modern barbecue classic. What makes this version special is the intricately flavored marinade, punctuated with the exuberance of mint, garlic, fresh lemon, and balsamic vinegar. Inhale and swoon.

Marinade

2 tablespoons chopped fresh rosemary

3 tablespoons chopped fresh mint

1/2 teaspoon ground black pepper

1 teaspoon salt

2 cloves garlic, minced

2 tablespoons honey or brown sugar

2 tablespoons fresh lemon juice

1 tablespoon balsamic vinegar

8 branches rosemary, about 10 inches long

1 1/2 pounds boneless leg of lamb, cut into
     1 1/2 -inch cubes

2 red bell peppers, seeded and cut into
     1 1/2 -inch squares

3 small zucchini, cut into 1/2 -inch-thick rounds

2 red onions, cut into wedges

Vegetable oil for the grill

on Rosemary Branches

1. Combine the marinade ingredients in a medium glass bowl. Set aside.

2. To make the rosemary skewers: Strip the leaves from the rosemary branches, leaving 2 inches of leaves at the tips. (Or use eight 10- to 12-inch bamboo skewers instead.)

3. Thread the lamb, bell pepper, zucchini, and onion alternately onto each of the branches or skewers. Place the kebabs in a baking dish, and cover with the marinade. Turn gently to coat. Let stand for 30 to 60 minutes in a cool place.

4. Meanwhile, prepare a medium-hot fire in a charcoal grill, or preheat a gas or electric grill to medium-high.

5. Brush the grill grate with vegetable oil. Remove the kebabs from the marinade; reserve the marinade for basting. Grill the kebabs until slightly charred or cooked as desired, about 5 to 7 minutes on each side for medium-rare, basting occasionally.

Serves 4

Tropical Fruit Salsa Tuna Sticks

We all crave homeostasis in our lives. These low-maintenance tuna kebabs, simply marinated and salsa-topped, are perfect for those days when it seems normal to park your head in a bag of Cheetos or ship yourself UPS to a tropical island. Eat. Drink. Hula. And don't call anyone in the morning.

Salsa

1 cup diced mango

1 cup diced pineapple

1 red bell pepper, seeded and chopped

1 jalapeño chile, seeded and minced

1/2 cup chopped red onion

2 tablespoons chopped fresh mint

2 tablespoons fresh lemon juice

Marinade

2 tablespoons honey or brown sugar

1/4 cup soy sauce

1/4 cup olive oil

2 teaspoons grated peeled fresh ginger

1 teaspoon Asian sesame oil

2 pounds tuna steak, cut into 2-inch cubes

Vegetable oil for the grill

1. Combine the salsa ingredients in a medium bowl. Cover and chill. Combine the marinade ingredients in a large glass bowl. Add the tuna. Cover and refrigerate for 30 minutes.

2. Soak eight 10- to 12-inch bamboo skewers in water for at least 30 minutes. Prepare a medium-hot fire in a charcoal grill, or preheat a gas or electric grill to medium-high.

3. With a slotted spoon, remove the fish from the marinade; reserve the marinade for basting. Thread the fish onto the skewers.

4. Brush the grill grate with vegetable oil. Grill the kebabs for 2 to 3 minutes on each side, basting occasionally. Ideally, the tuna should still be red-rare in the center. Serve with the salsa.

Serves 4

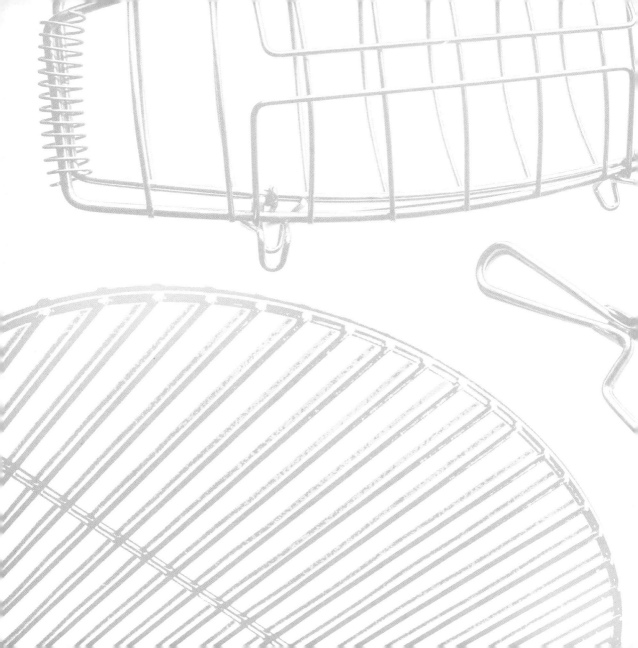

CHAPTER 3

The Big Heat

Smoldering centerpieces—raw intensity and drama, getting down and dangerous with meat and fish

Big Daddy's High-Style Cheese-Stuffed Burgers

This is the kind of dish Albert Collins had on his mind when he sang, "Just 'cause you're hungry and happen to come in late, don't you go reachin' across *my* plate." In this update on cheeseburgers and ketchup, plump burgers ooze hot drips and splotches of sun-dried tomato paste and imported Swiss, lovingly tucked inside the patty before it's grilled. They're the perfect excuse for putting aside everything your mama taught you about sharing. Who's gonna tell?

1 1/2 pounds ground beef chuck

Salt and ground black pepper to taste

3/4 cup shredded Gruyère cheese

1/4 cup sun-dried tomato paste

Vegetable oil for the grill

4 hamburger buns or kaiser rolls

Mayonnaise and mustard for serving

1 medium red onion, thinly sliced

1 small head Bibb lettuce, separated into leaves

1. Prepare a medium-hot fire in a charcoal grill, or preheat a gas or electric grill to medium-high.

2. Season the beef with salt and pepper. Divide into 4 portions. Divide 1 portion in half and form each half into a 4-inch patty slightly thicker in the center than at the edges. Repeat with the remaining 3 portions, for a total of 8 patties. Top 4 of the patties with the shredded cheese, leaving a 1/4-inch border. Spread 1 tablespoon of the sun-dried tomato paste over the cheese. Top with the remaining patties, pinching the edges together to seal. Transfer to a tray. Cover with plastic wrap and refrigerate until ready to grill.

3. Brush the grill grate with vegetable oil. Grill the patties (covering the grill only if using a gas grill), turning only once, until they reach the desired doneness, 3 to 4 minutes total for medium-rare. The burgers will continue to cook slightly after being removed from the grill.

4. Place the buns, cut side down, on the grill for about 15 seconds to lightly toast them. Spread mayonnaise and mustard on the buns, and then assemble the burgers, adding onion slices and lettuce.

Serves 4

Cowboy Church Sunday School

Get ready for the three stages of ribdom: anticipation, temptation, and salvation. True believers know that pork ribs are the only path to barbecue glory—here paved with its own Mexican-Chinese-Deep Southern juju: a devilish chipotle-honey paste, a sauce full of whiskey fire, and celestial heat throughout. The recipe is named after the 1955 hit by the Cowboy Church Sunday School band, 'cause we're certain you'll "Open Up Your Heart" to its sinful pleasures. Our advice: Eat first, confess later.

Spice Paste

3 tablespoons honey

2 teaspoons salt

$1^1/2$ tablespoons sweet paprika

2 teaspoons chipotle paste or ground chile powder

$1/2$ teaspoon ground nutmeg

1 teaspoon ground cumin

1 teaspoon Chinese five-spice powder

1 tablespoon ground ginger

1 tablespoon Worcestershire sauce

3 tablespoons olive oil

2 to $2^1/2$ slabs baby back ribs (4 to 5 pounds total)

Bourbon Barbecue Sauce

$1/2$ cup tomato ketchup

2 ounces ($1/4$ cup) bourbon

1 tablespoon Worcestershire sauce

1 teaspoon Dijon mustard

1 tablespoon each: minced garlic and minced peeled fresh ginger

$1/4$ cup firmly packed dark brown sugar

3 tablespoons cider vinegar

$1/3$ cup water

$1/2$ teaspoon red pepper flakes

Salt and ground black pepper to taste

Vegetable oil for the grill

Ribs with Righteous Bourbon Sauce

1. To make the spice paste: In a food processor, combine the spice paste ingredients and process to a paste.

2. Line a heavy-duty baking pan with a double layer of aluminum foil. Coat the bottom of the pan with the olive oil. Pat the ribs dry, then rub all over with the paste. Place in the baking pan, cover tightly with foil, and refrigerate for at least 5 hours or overnight.

3. Let the ribs come to room temperature (still wrapped in foil), about 30 minutes.

4. Put an oven rack in the middle position and preheat the oven to 350°F. Bake the foil-covered ribs until the meat is just tender and begins to pull away from the ends of the bones, about 1$\frac{1}{2}$ hours. (You can bake the ribs up to 1 day ahead and refrigerate until ready to grill.)

5. Meanwhile, make the barbecue sauce: Combine the sauce ingredients in a small saucepan over moderate heat. Simmer, uncovered, stirring occasionally, until medium thick, 15 to 20 minutes.

6. Prepare a medium fire in a charcoal grill, or preheat a gas or electric grill to medium. Brush the grill grate with vegetable oil.

7. Transfer the ribs to an area of the grill with no coals underneath, reserving the pan juices. Cover the grill and cook until the ribs are tender and browned, about 30 to 40 minutes total, basting the ribs generously with the pan juices and barbecue sauce and turning them every 7 to 10 minutes. Transfer to a cutting board and let stand for 5 minutes before cutting between the ribs to separate them.

Serves 4 to 6

Get Down to It Skirt Steak

Sure, skirt steak is a bit high on the chewy quotient, and it needs a blast of high heat for the full combustion. But when hot-wired with chiles, cumin, and cilantro and grilled just right, it elicits the kind of animal grunts usually reserved for watching vintage clips of James Brown, the Godfather of Soul, wailing like a gladiator in a skin-tight suit. Feel good *and* super bad by stashing the leftovers in pita pocket bread with mayo and lettuce.

1 1/4 pounds skirt steak, preferably Angus beef

3 tablespoons Demonic Flavor Booster (page 18)

1 1/2 teaspoons kosher salt

Vegetable oil for the grill

1. Prepare a hot fire in a charcoal grill, or preheat a gas or electric grill to high.

2. Rub the steak all over with Demonic Flavor Booster. Sprinkle with salt. Set aside on a plate and let sit at room temperature for 30 minutes.

3. Brush the grill grate with vegetable oil. Place the steak over the hot fire. Grill, turning once, until the steak is the desired doneness: 7 to 8 minutes for medium-rare, 10 minutes for medium. Transfer to a cutting board and let rest for 3 minutes before serving.

Serves 4

Wicked Indonesian

A backyard dish inspired by the four major food groups: protein, sugar, peanut butter, and booze. All this, plus a sauce that is edgier than a late-night bash in Bali. This bird is meant for the grill-seeker willing to orbit way above the usual chicken feed. On the side? Just sliced cukes and grilled baguette slices, plus Grilled Cardamom Nectarines (page 86) to close the deal.

Sauce

3/4 cup creamy peanut butter

1 1/2 ounces (3 tablespoons) Scotch whisky

2 tablespoons soy sauce

2/3 cup fresh lemon juice (4 lemons)

3 tablespoons brown sugar

3 large cloves garlic, minced

1 teaspoon red pepper flakes

3/4 cup water

6 boneless chicken breast halves, skins left on

Salt and ground black pepper to taste

Vegetable oil for the grill

Chopped peeled fresh ginger for garnish

Chicken with Whisky Peanut Sauce

1. Prepare a medium-hot fire in a charcoal grill, or preheat a gas or electric grill to medium-high.

2. To make the sauce: In a small, heavy saucepan, combine the sauce ingredients and bring to a boil over medium heat. Stir until smooth. Remove from the heat, cover, and keep warm.

3. Pat the chicken breasts dry, and season with salt and pepper. Brush the grill grate with vegetable oil. Place the chicken, skin side down, on the grate. Grill, turning once, until just cooked through, about 10 minutes.

4. Transfer to a carving board and let rest for 5 minutes. Cut lengthwise into thin slices. Arrange on a heated platter, and drizzle with the sauce. Garnish with chopped ginger.

Serves 6

Dig This Pig

Nothing contributes to your backyard creds more than a classy pig feed. This one is all about the skin-deep mash-up of fresh herbs, mustard, and the caramelized, near-burnt tones of fruit preserves, all clinging to loins of pork with a sweet, deep squeal. Spoon a spiffy fruit salsa on top to up the wow factor. And if you really want to display your barbecue savoir faire, brine the pork in advance (see page 28).

Spice Paste

2 cloves garlic, minced

2 tablespoons finely chopped fresh rosemary

2 tablespoons thyme

1 tablespoon peach or apricot preserves

1 tablespoon minced lemon zest

1 tablespoon Dijon mustard

3 tablespoons olive oil

2 teaspoons each: salt and ground black pepper

2 pounds pork tenderloin, trimmed of silver skin

Vegetable oil for the grill

Peach and Sweet Onion Jamba (page 23) or your favorite chutney for serving

1. Prepare a medium-hot fire in a charcoal grill, or preheat a gas or electric grill to medium-high.

2. To make the paste: Combine the paste ingredients in a small bowl. Rub over the pork and let stand for 5 to 7 minutes.

3. Brush the grill grate with vegetable oil. Grill the pork, turning to brown all sides, until it reaches an internal temperature of 145°F, about 15 to 20 minutes. Remove the pork and let rest for 10 to 15 minutes. Cut into 1/2-inch-thick slices and arrange on a platter. Serve warm or at room temperature with the fruit salsa or chutney.

Serves 6

Male Bonding Beer-Brined Chicken

When the guys get together, matching silverware and other civilized pretensions don't factor. What counts is immediacy and flexibility, the kind of flavor-intensive food you can throw together without calling mom, then brag on when the gang shows up. This feisty chicken goes the distance, right down to a beer brine that will bring the bird to its tender-loving knees. Cheers.

1 chicken, 3 1/2 to 4 pounds, butterflied by your butcher

The Best Beer Brine (page 28)

3 tablespoons olive oil

Fire + Salt Caramel-Fennel Rub (page 22)

Vegetable oil for the grill

1. Put the chicken in a large glass bowl and pour the brine over it. If the bird is not completely covered, add some cold water. Refrigerate, covered, for 4 hours.

2. Remove the chicken from the brine and pat dry with paper towels. Rub both sides with the olive oil, and sprinkle with the rub mixture. Let sit for 30 minutes.

3. Prepare a medium-hot fire in a charcoal grill, or preheat a gas or electric grill to medium-high. For a charcoal grill, when the coals are covered with a white-gray ash, divide them into 2 piles and set a drip pan between the piles.

4. Brush the grill grate with vegetable oil. Place the chicken, skin side up, in the center of the grill (not directly over the heat). Cover and cook, turning every 10 minutes, until the juices run clear and a meat thermometer inserted in the thickest part of the thigh registers 175°F, about 40 to 50 minutes. Let rest for 10 minutes before cutting into quarters and serving.

Serves 4

Superhero Sesame-Ginger Tuna

The master of the grill universe defends tuna's core flavor, keeping the center moist and medium-rare. We're treading lightly here, adding a taste of Asian soul, which throws down just the right luster. Nothing combustible, just a wash of healthy flavors to get tongues shaking.

4 tuna steaks, each about 1 inch thick

1/2 cup Asian sesame oil

1/2 cup soy sauce

1 tablespoon rice wine vinegar

1 tablespoon finely grated peeled fresh ginger

Vegetable oil for the grill

Coarsely ground black pepper to taste

1/2 teaspoon finely chopped green onion
(green part only) for garnish

1. Arrange the tuna steaks in a flat glass baking dish. Brush both sides with some of the sesame oil.

2. Combine the remaining sesame oil with the soy sauce, vinegar, and ginger in a small bowl. Pour over the tuna steaks and marinate at room temperature for 20 to 30 minutes, turning several times.

3. Meanwhile, prepare a hot fire in a charcoal grill, or preheat a gas or electric grill to high.

4. Brush the grill grate with vegetable oil. Remove the tuna from the marinade and crank coarsely ground pepper on each side. Discard the marinade. Grill the tuna for 2 minutes on each side to sear the steaks. Move to a medium-heat spot (for a charcoal grill), or reduce the heat to medium (for a gas or electric grill). Grill 2 to 3 more minutes per side for rare, 5 to 6 minutes per side for medium. Use a wide metal spatula to turn the steaks, and rotate the fish 45 degrees when halfway done on each side, for crosshatch grill marks.

5. Garnish with green onion and serve.

Serves 4

Black-Peppered Maple Salmon

In this Vermont-meets-Shanghai salmon grill, butter-soft fish combines with the sweetness of maple syrup and the Asian undertow of ginger and soy. The deep immersion in the marinade ensures that the manifold principle of Chinese cuisine is in full force—a marriage of sweet and soy, hot and oily, that coats the salmon with a harmonious glaze, replacing fishiness with finesse and flavor. The idea comes by way of New Jersey, cooked up by our food-loving friends Brad and Mary Harmon.

Marinade

1 cup soy sauce

1 cup maple syrup

1 teaspoon minced peeled fresh ginger

4 to 6 salmon fillets, 6 ounces each, skin removed

1/4 cup coarsely ground black pepper

Vegetable oil for the grill

1. Combine the marinade ingredients in a small bowl and stir until smooth.

2. Put the salmon in a large, resealable plastic bag and add the marinade to cover the fillets. Refrigerate for 4 to 24 hours, turning once or twice.

3. Prepare a medium-low to medium fire in a charcoal grill, or preheat a gas or electric grill to medium-low or medium.

4. Remove the fillets and blot the excess marinade with paper towels. Lightly dust one side of each with ground pepper until you have an even coat, pressing it into the fish so it adheres. Discard the marinade.

5. Brush the grill grate with vegetable oil. Place the salmon on the grill, pepper side up. Grill, turning once or twice, until cooked through and firm but still moist, about 5 to 7 minutes. Do not overcook.

Serves 4 to 6
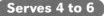

CHAPTER 4

Side Shows

Crazy-delicious diversions to go with everything

Thyme-Bomb Red Onions

Sweet-and-Sour Caramelized Onions

Burning Spears

Cowgirl Love Vegetable Roundup

The Ginger-Lime Coleslaw Revolution

Cheesy Grilled Corn with Basil Butter

Seared Romaine Salad with Garlic-Parmesan Sparks

Le Hot French Caprese Salad

Thyme-Bomb Red Onions

Eau de onion. It's the essential scent of a barbecue, perfuming entire blocks and making grown men cry—with joy. But make no mistake: These are not your father's grilled onions. We're going full bore here, soaking the onion hunks in lemon juice and thyme, then searing and basting them until outrageously delicious. Bring on the steaks!

1 tablespoon chopped fresh thyme

1 tablespoon grated lemon zest

Juice of 1 large lemon, strained

1/2 teaspoon red pepper flakes

1/2 cup olive oil

Salt and ground black pepper to taste

6 red onions, peeled and cut in half lengthwise

Vegetable oil for the grill

1. In a glass bowl, combine the thyme, lemon zest and juice, pepper flakes, oil, and salt and pepper. Add the onions and marinate for 2 hours, turning occasionally.

2. Meanwhile, prepare a medium fire in a charcoal grill, or preheat a gas or electric grill to medium.

3. Brush a grill basket or the grill grate with vegetable oil. Arrange the onions in the basket or directly on the grill grate. Grill over glowing coals until tender and browned, 6 to 8 minutes on each side, brushing with the marinade halfway through. Serve immediately.

Serves 6

Sweet-and-Sour Caramelized Onions

Here little sweet onions are simmered in a sugar-vinegar bath until the juices run thick, tart, and sweeter than the day you tell your boss, "I'm outta this rat hole." If there's a more perfect, more comforting sidekick to a hunk of steer, pork, or game, we haven't found it.

2 tablespoons unsalted butter

2 tablespoons olive oil

1 1/2 tablespoons sugar

1/3 cup high-quality balsamic vinegar

2 pounds cipollini or small onions, peeled and rinsed

1/2 teaspoon each: salt and ground black pepper

Chopped fresh mint leaves or parsley for garnish

1. In a large saucepan over medium heat, melt the butter into the olive oil. Stir in the sugar and keep stirring until it dissolves. Lower the heat, add the vinegar, and boil the mixture for 3 minutes to reduce it slightly.

2. Add the onions, salt, and pepper, stirring to coat the onions evenly with the sauce. Cover and cook over low heat, stirring occasionally, until a toothpick easily pierces the onions, 30 to 40 minutes. The vinegar will thicken and have a consistency like maple syrup. If it gets too thick, add some water.

3. Serve warm or at room temperature, garnished with mint or parsley.

Serves 6

Burning Spears

Forget all that voodoo about peeling asparagus and standing them at attention in a pot of steaming water. Instead, just slick the spears with olive oil, garlic, and pepper heat. Then pop them on a heated grill until hot, crunchy, and blackened at the edges.

3 tablespoons olive oil

2 teaspoons minced garlic

3/4 teaspoon red pepper flakes

1 teaspoon kosher salt

1 pound large asparagus, woody ends trimmed

Vegetable oil for the grill

1 teaspoon fresh lemon juice

⟶ Thin asparagus may fall through the grate during cooking. Use an oiled grill basket if necessary.

1. Prepare a medium fire in a charcoal grill, or preheat a gas or electric grill to medium.

2. In a shallow baking dish, combine the oil, garlic, pepper flakes, and salt. Toss the asparagus in the seasoned oil to coat evenly.

3. Brush the grill grate with vegetable oil. Place the asparagus on the grate in a single layer. Grill, turning every 2 to 3 minutes, until grill-marked and tender, 10 to 15 minutes. Transfer to a plate, sprinkle with the lemon juice, and serve.

Serves 4

Cowgirl Love Vegetable

Side dishes, like relationships, are best when they're uncomplicated. Leave the drama to the entrees and over-the-top desserts. The advantage of this recipe, a simple sear of zukes and peppers with enough dark, sweet vinegar to get lips smacking, is that it marries well with just about anything except a lone ranger. Saddle up.

Roundup

4 large yellow bell peppers

3 zucchini

$1/2$ cup olive oil

$1/4$ cup balsamic vinegar

$1 1/2$ teaspoons dried herbes de
   Provence

$1 1/2$ teaspoons salt

Ground black pepper to taste

Vegetable oil for the grill

1. Prepare a medium-hot fire in a char-coal grill, or preheat a gas or electric grill to medium-high. Seed the peppers and cut lengthwise into 2-inch-wide strips. Cut the zucchini lengthwise into $1/4$-inch-thick strips.

2. In a flat baking dish, combine the peppers and zucchini. Pour the olive oil and balsamic vinegar over them, and sprinkle with the herbs, salt, and pepper to taste. Toss to coat well and set aside.

3. Brush a grill basket or the grill grate with vegetable oil. Grill the vegetables, turning frequently, until browned and tender, 8 to 10 minutes. Serve warm or at room temperature.

Serves 6

The Ginger-Lime Coleslaw Revolution

This Asian update on the green theme is more complex than Chinese capitalism. It's snappy and sweet, hot and limey, gingery and extra crunchy with green onions. We love a good mayonnaise-trashy coleslaw, but this version is a great leap forward.

Dressing

1/3 cup sugar

1/3 cup rice wine vinegar or white vinegar

1/3 cup vegetable oil

1/4 cup fresh lime juice

1 tablespoon minced peeled fresh ginger

1 cup thinly sliced green onions (green and white parts)

2 teaspoons Asian sesame oil

2 tablespoons hot sauce

2 tablespoons kosher salt

Ground black pepper to taste

1 large head green cabbage, cored and finely chopped (about 10 cups)

4 carrots, peeled and finely grated

1. In a large serving bowl, combine the dressing ingredients. Whisk well. Add the cabbage and carrots and toss thoroughly. Serve at room temperature.

Serves 6 to 8

Cheesy Grilled Corn with Basil Butter

The cure for fresh corn fatigue: Char the ears in their husks, strip them naked, then roll them in soft butter spiked with basil and lemon. For a final flourish, hit the glistening rows with a flurry of grated Parmesan.

6 ears corn, husks on

1 stick (8 tablespoons) unsalted butter, softened

1 tablespoon fresh lemon juice

1 tablespoon chopped fresh basil

Salt and ground black pepper to taste

Vegetable oil for the grill

$1/2$ cup freshly grated Parmesan cheese

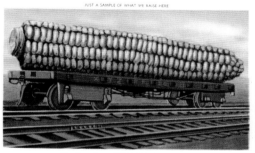

Greetings from STACYVILLE, MAINE

1. Soak the corn in a large bowl of water for 1 hour (so the husks don't catch fire).

2. Prepare a medium-hot fire in a charcoal grill, or preheat a gas or electric grill to medium-high.

3. In a small bowl, mix the butter with the lemon juice and basil, and season with salt and pepper. Spread out the butter in a $1/4$-inch-thick layer in the center of a large plate or baking sheet and set aside.

4. Brush the grill grate with vegetable oil. Grill the corn, turning often, until the husks are evenly charred all over, 25 to 30 minutes. Carefully peel back the corn husks, but leave them attached to the cobs. Discard the corn silk and use the husks as handles. Roll the corn in the softened butter, and top with Parmesan cheese. Serve immediately.

Serves 6

Seared Romaine Salad with

If you want to woo a date or chew with the heavy hitters, you've got to address the Caesar salad issue. That means thinking beyond torn leaves and treating garlic and anchovy like something more than a sleeper cell. Our suggestion: Grill whole heads of romaine until warm, slightly wilty, and touched with charred splendor, then dress with attitude in every bite.

Dressing

4 cloves garlic, minced

1 teaspoon Dijon mustard

1 1/2 tablespoons mayonnaise

2 teaspoons grated lemon zest

1 tablespoon fresh lemon juice

1 teaspoon Worcestershire sauce

4 anchovy fillets

1 cup olive oil, plus more if needed

2 tablespoons white wine vinegar

Salt and ground black pepper to taste

2 heads romaine lettuce, halved lengthwise

2 tablespoons olive oil

Salt and ground black pepper to taste

Vegetable oil for the grill

One 2-ounce piece Parmesan cheese, shaved into strips with
   a vegetable peeler

Garlic-Parmesan Sparks

1. Prepare a medium-low fire in a charcoal grill, or preheat a gas or electric grill to medium-low.

2. To make the dressing: In a food processor, blend the garlic, mustard, mayonnaise, lemon zest and juice, Worcestershire sauce, and anchovies. With the motor running, slowly add the oil in a stream through the feed tube, and then the vinegar. Season with salt and pepper. If too thick, add more olive oil.

3. Brush the romaine halves with the 2 tablespoons of olive oil and season with salt and pepper. Brush the grill grate with vegetable oil. Put the lettuce, cut side down, directly over the heat. Grill, turning occasionally, until the outer leaves are charred and wilted and the lettuce is warm and just barely tender, 2 to 5 minutes. Put the lettuce on a plate and let rest for 5 minutes.

4. Place half a head of romaine, cut side up, on each plate. Drizzle with dressing and top with Parmesan shavings.

Serves 4

L'ÉTÉ À
MONTE CARLO BEACH
C'EST LE SOLEIL, LE SOLEIL ...

Le Hot

What do you get when you stack up slices of grilled eggplant, fresh tomatoes, and creamy buffalo mozzarella and then hit the whole thing with a vinaigrette and fresh basil? A cross between a savory French Napoleon pastry and an Italian caprese salad. Now that's classy.

French Caprese Salad

2 medium eggplants

$1/2$ cup olive oil

Salt and ground black pepper to taste

Vegetable oil for the grill

4 large tomatoes, sliced $1/4$ inch thick

4 fresh buffalo mozzarella balls, sliced $1/4$ inch thick

2 tablespoons balsamic vinegar

3 tablespoons chopped fresh basil

1. Prepare a medium-hot fire in a charcoal grill, or preheat a gas or electric grill to medium-high.

2. Remove the stems from the eggplants, and cut crosswise into $1/4$-inch-thick slices. Brush with 3 tablespoons of the olive oil, and season with salt and pepper.

3. Brush the grill grate with vegetable oil. Grill the eggplant slices until grill-marked and fairly soft, 8 to 10 minutes, brushing with another 2 tablespoons of the olive oil and turning frequently.

4. On a serving platter, make 6 stacks, alternating slices of grilled eggplant, tomato, and mozzarella. Sprinkle the tops with the remaining 3 tablespoons of olive oil, the balsamic vinegar, and basil. Finish with a little salt and pepper.

Serves 6

CHAPTER 5

Cocktails with the transforming tendency of fizz, fruit, and fantasy

Mr. Lucky

Finding the right cocktail to kick off an intimate outdoor dinner party is a higher calling. It must be manly but stylish, accessible but slightly dangerous, with the power to seduce the seen-it-all palate. We think our gin and muddled mint cooler, topped off with sparkling grapefruit taste, hits just the right notes. It's bright, clean, frontal, and totally refreshing. We're fond of the tartly delicious Izze grapefruit drink found at boutique grocery stores—it's worth seeking out. When squeezing the grapefruit, be sure to scrape in lots of pulpy shreds to add body and a lip-smacking chew. For maximum flavor, it's best to make these individually, but if you want a batch, multiply and go for it.

3 tablespoons fresh pink grapefruit juice

10 to 15 small fresh mint leaves (about 2 tablespoons)

Ice cubes

2 ounces (1/4 cup) gin

Chilled Izze Grapefruit or other carbonated grapefruit drink

Mint sprig for garnish

1. Pour the grapefruit juice into the bottom of a wide-mouthed, heavy-bottomed glass or a glass measuring cup. Add the mint and, with a muddler or the handle of a wooden spoon, gently muddle the leaves to release their flavor.

2. Pour the muddled grapefruit juice and mint into a highball or pilsner glass. Fill the glass almost to the top with ice cubes. Pour in the gin and stir quickly and briskly to chill.

3. Add enough sparkling grapefruit drink to fill the glass, and give a quick stir. Pop in a mint sprig and serve.

Serves 1

Jazzed-Out Blackberry-Thyme Mojitos

Think hot. Think thirsty. Think desperate. Now think satisfaction, as this sensuous drink reaches your lips and cools the throat without chilling your fire. Our mojito formula comes with a bebop blackberry aura and its own earthy intrigue: the herbal thrust of thyme to dance with the traditional mint. Pineapple juice, the finishing splash, adds another dreamy dimension. Use organic if possible; it's more concentrated and less sweet.

3/4 cup fresh lime juice (6 to 7 limes)

3/4 cup sugar or simple syrup (see page 82)

1/2 cup loosely packed fresh mint leaves

8 thyme sprigs, each about 2 1/2 inches long

12 blackberries, fresh or frozen and thawed

Ice cubes

12 ounces (1 1/2 cups) white rum

3/4 cup pineapple juice

Chilled club soda

6 mint sprigs for garnish

1. Combine the lime juice, sugar or simple syrup, mint, thyme, and blackberries in a large serving pitcher. With a muddler or the handle of a long wooden spoon, mash gently until the sugar is dissolved in the lime juice, the flavors of the herbs are released, and the blackberries are crushed.

2. When ready to serve, fill the pitcher with ice cubes. Add the rum and pineapple juice, stirring quickly and briskly to chill. Top off the mixture with a big splash of club soda.

3. Strain into ice-filled rock glasses. Garnish each drink with a mint sprig.

Serves 6

BBQ Banana Daiquiri

Sure, this sounds like a crazy way to close out the barbecue party. Smear whole, slit-open bananas with brown sugar and orange liqueur and grill them until they take on their own soft, charred, custardy buzz. Put them in a blender with the rum-soaked fixings for a daiquiri. Pulverize the whole thing into nectar more decadent than ancient Rome. Mash it through a strainer into cocktail glasses and hit the surface with a little cinnamon and a few cracks of black pepper. Two words: reckless and divine. What are you waitin' for?

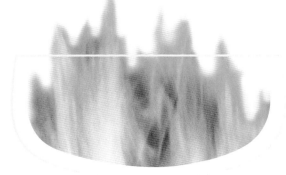

Barbecued Bananas

2 unpeeled ripe bananas

1/4 cup firmly packed brown sugar

1 ounce (2 tablespoons) Cointreau or orange liqueur

4 ounces (1/2 cup) dark rum

1 ounce (2 tablespoons) Cointreau or orange liqueur

1/4 cup fresh lime juice

2 cups cracked ice

Ground cinnamon and freshly cracked black pepper for garnish

1. Prepare a medium-hot fire in a charcoal grill, or preheat a gas or electric grill to medium-high.

2. To barbecue the bananas: With a sharp knife, cut a slit lengthwise through each banana, cutting through the skin and going just deep enough to spread the banana open slightly. Pack each banana with 2 tablespoons of the brown sugar, then drizzle 1/2 ounce (1 tablespoon) of Cointreau into each sugar-stuffed banana.

3. Grill the bananas, cut side up, for 10 minutes, or until the fruit has softened and separated slightly from the peel, and is slightly caramelized. Remove and set aside to cool for a couple of minutes.

4. To make the drinks: Scoop the softened fruit into a blender (discard the banana peels). Add the rum, Cointreau, lime juice, and cracked ice. Blend until smooth. Strain the mixture through a strainer into 4 cocktail glasses. Garnish each drink with a good shake of cinnamon and some cracked black pepper.

Serves 4

The X-treme Dark 'n' Stormy

Imagine Joe Pesci, Mr. *GoodFellas* himself, stirring things up in the yard in the steam of summer. Meaning: This is no simple dark 'n' stormy, a throw-down drink of dark rum and ginger beer. It's the edge of night, jumped up with ginger powder and a heap of lime, cranked with orange tones, and then powered by bottles of extra ginger beer, just to make it fun. What can we say? It's a killer drink.

3/4 cup fresh lime juice (6 to 7 limes)

2 limes, cut into 1/2-inch wedges

2 large oranges, 1 cut into 1/2-inch wedges and 1 cut into 8 thin slices for garnish

1/2 to 1 teaspoon ground ginger

1/2 cup sugar or simple syrup (see page 82)

16 ounces (2 cups) dark rum

4 chilled 12-ounce bottles ginger beer, preferably Reed's Extra Ginger

Ice cubes

1. Combine the lime juice, lime and orange wedges, ginger, and sugar or simple syrup in a large pitcher. With a muddler or the handle of a long wooden spoon, gently mash until the ginger and sugar are dissolved in the lime juice and the pulp is released from the fruit wedges.

2. Add the rum, then gently stir in the ginger beer.

3. Fill 8 rocks glasses with ice, strain the mixture into the glasses, and tuck an orange slice into each glass to garnish.

Serves 8

Lascivious Limon Drops

Guys tend to like lemon drops but the girls l-o-v-e 'em. Vodka, lots of fresh lemons, an elegant sugar rim—all tasting like a glam lemonade. Our swanky friend Michael Freeman, known for his martini savvy, has slyly sharpened the formula with lots of fresh lime. The result? A lemon-lime or "limon" drop, designed to make you the kind of mixmaster men want to be—and women want to be with.

Simple Syrup

1 cup water

1 cup granulated sugar

Sugar Rims (optional)

1/2 cup superfine sugar

6 lemon wedges

2/3 cup fresh lemon juice (4 lemons)

2/3 cup lime juice (5 to 6 limes)

12 ounces (1 1/2 cups) vodka

Ice cubes

1. To make the syrup: In a small saucepan, bring the water to a boil. Remove from the heat, stir in the granulated sugar, and continue stirring until completely dissolved. Set aside to cool.

2. To make the rims, if you wish: Put the superfine sugar in a deep, wide bowl. Make a slit in the center of a lemon wedge and center the cut wedge on the rim of a 4-ounce cocktail glass. Run the wedge around the rim, lightly squeezing to moisten the rim. Tip the bowl at an angle and quickly twirl the rim in the sugar to make a nice, wide band. Repeat with 5 more glasses. Chill the glasses until ready to serve.

3. To serve: Pour the simple syrup, lemon juice, lime juice, and vodka into a large pitcher filled with ice cubes. Stir quickly and briskly to chill. Strain into the sugar-rimmed glasses and serve.

Serves 6

Those Fabulous Fruit Stand Tequila Sippers

Here's a twist on the whole infused cocktail thing, guy-style. All you need is a bottle of good tequila, fresh fruit (feel free to cut loose on variations), and a big, *clean* glass jar (yeah, we're talking to *you*). Add a vanilla bean for yummy fragrance, ginger for attitude, and brown sugar to sweeten the deal. Let sit for a week, then shake it over ice into cocktail glasses garnished with fresh fruit. Mercy!

1 pint fresh ripe strawberries, hulled

1/2 small pineapple, peeled and chopped

One 2-inch piece fresh ginger, peeled and sliced

1 vanilla bean, split lengthwise

2 tablespoons brown sugar or simple syrup (see page 82)

One 750-ml bottle best-quality gold or silver tequila

Garnishes

Eight 2-inch pineapple wedges

8 strawberries

Cracked ice or ice cubes

1. Combine all the ingredients except the garnishes in a large, clean glass container with an airtight lid. Let sit in a dark place for 1 week, stirring the mixture at least a couple of times during the infusion.

2. To serve: Strain the infused tequila into a clean jar. To chill, shake the tequila quickly and vigorously—about one third of it at a time—in a cocktail shaker half-filled with cracked ice or ice cubes. Strain into chilled martini glasses. To garnish: With a plastic toothpick sword, skewer a pineapple wedge and a strawberry for each drink and drop into the glass.

Serves 8

CHAPTER 6

How to grill your cake and eat it, too

Grilled Cardamom Nectarines

Roasted Banana Splits

S'mores Cake

Beastie Bars

Chocolate-Blasted, Caramel-Drippin' Turtle Sundaes

Emergency Grilled Pound Cake Extravaganza

Screamin' Berry Ice Cream Sandwiches

Grilled Cardamon Nectarines

This is not your mother's grilled peaches and vanilla ice cream. These babies have their own Euro-India-groove— massaged with brown sugar and the sweet, pungent intrigue of cardamom, all grilled to a final glory. A scoop of dulce de leche adds a creamy-cold, burnt-caramel finish. Chic, easy, unexpected.

6 ripe but firm nectarines, halved and pitted

2 tablespoons olive oil

1 tablespoon light brown sugar

1/2 teaspoon ground cardamom

Vegetable oil for the grill

1 pint dulce de leche ice cream

1. Prepare a medium fire in a charcoal grill, or preheat a gas or electric grill to medium.

2. Put the nectarines in a large bowl, and sprinkle with the olive oil, brown sugar, and cardamom. Mix gently.

3. Brush the grill grate with vegetable oil. Grill the nectarines directly over the fire, cut side down, until grill marks are visible, about 5 minutes. Turn the fruit over and grill until grill marks show and the nectarines are tender, 4 to 5 minutes more. Serve 2 nectarine halves in each bowl, topped with a scoop of ice cream.

Serves 6

Roasted Banana Splits

"What doesn't kill me makes me stronger," said Friedrich Nietzsche. Consider the German philosopher's astute observation when you dig into this unconscionably rich upgrade of the soda fountain classic: grilled, rum-buttered bananas blitzed with coffee ice cream, chocolate, and toasted coconut shreds.

3 tablespoons unsalted butter

2 tablespoons light brown sugar

2 ounces (1/4 cup) dark rum

4 ripe but firm bananas

Vegetable oil for the grill

1 pint high-quality coffee ice cream

1/2 cup grated semisweet chocolate

1/2 cup sweetened shredded coconut, toasted (see Note)

→ To toast coconut, spread it out on a baking sheet and bake in a 350°F oven, stirring occasionally, for 10 to 15 minutes, until golden brown and crisp.

1. Prepare a medium fire in a charcoal grill, or preheat a gas or electric grill to medium.

2. In a small saucepan over low heat, melt the butter. Add the brown sugar and rum, and stir until the sugar dissolves.

3. Peel the bananas, and cut them in half lengthwise. Place in a large, shallow baking pan, in one layer. Brush gently on both sides with the warm rum mixture.

4. Brush the grill grate with vegetable oil. Using a metal spatula, place the bananas directly over the fire, cut side down. Grill until browned, about 2 minutes on each side. (You can grill the bananas on only one side if they are difficult to handle.)

5. For each serving, place 2 banana halves on a dessert plate and top with a scoop of ice cream. Sprinkle with grated chocolate and toasted coconut.

Serves 4

S'mores Cake

Campground cuisine goes full throttle in this grill-cooked cake from our food-savvy friend Lena Lencek. S'mores' holy trinity—grahams, chocolate, and marshmallows—is layered in a square foil wrapper, then heated over hot coals. When the whole thing is hot, melty, and oozy, spoon on clouds of espresso-fueled whipped cream. Troop 49 never had it so good.

One 1-pound box graham crackers

1 pound high-quality bittersweet chocolate, coarsely chopped

1 pound marshmallows

2 cups heavy cream

5 tablespoons confectioners' sugar

1/4 teaspoon finely ground instant espresso powder

1 teaspoon vanilla extract

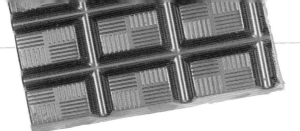

1. Prepare a medium fire in a charcoal grill, or preheat a gas or electric grill to medium. Line an 8 1/2-inch square baking dish with 2 overlapping 18-inch-long sheets of aluminum foil, one vertical and the other horizontal, centering the 2 sheets so that they extend about 5 inches beyond the edge of the baking dish on each side.

2. Place a single layer of graham crackers in the pan. Top with a layer of chocolate pieces, and then a layer of marshmallows. Repeat until you have no more ingredients left, ending with a layer of marshmallows.

3. Fold the aluminum foil over the top, and crimp the edges. Carefully lift the cake from the pan and transfer to the grill. Cook until the marshmallows and chocolate pieces are melted, about 15 to 20 minutes.

4. Meanwhile, in a chilled bowl, whip the heavy cream until stiff peaks form, then whip in the confectioners' sugar, espresso powder, and vanilla extract.

5. Transfer the foil packet to a serving platter. Unwrap the cake, cut into squares, and serve with the whipped cream.

Serves 6

Beastie Bars

They're part brownie, part candy bar, and all old-school heaven. But the real beauty of these little squares of post-barbecue badness? They're easy (if you can turn on the oven and dump ingredients into a pan, you're there) and flexible (swap in your favorite chips, or sub cookies for the grahams). Perfect for those days when you need to put some bling in your baking.

4 whole graham crackers

4 tablespoons unsalted butter, melted

$1/2$ cup sweetened shredded coconut

$1/2$ cup semisweet chocolate chips

$1/2$ cup white chocolate chips

$3/4$ cup sweetened condensed milk

$1/2$ cup chopped walnuts or pecans

Ground cinnamon to taste

1. Preheat the oven to 350°F.

2. In a blender or food processor, reduce the graham crackers to crumbs. Measure out 1 cup, and discard the rest.

3. Combine the crumbs and melted butter, and press into the bottom of an 8-inch square baking pan. Sprinkle the coconut evenly over the crust. Add the semisweet chocolate chips in one layer and top with the white chocolate chips. Pour the condensed milk evenly over the chips. Top with the nuts, gently pressing them halfway into the condensed milk. Sprinkle a little cinnamon on top.

4. Bake for 25 to 30 minutes, or until the condensed milk sets. Cool completely. Cut into small squares to serve.

Makes 16 squares

Chocolate-Blasted, Caramel-Drippin' Turtle Sundaes

Turtles, those retro-iffic candy clusters of chocolate, caramel, and nuts, are the inspiration here. We simply deconstructed the elements and repackaged them into something new and wonderfully wicked: great chunks of toasted pecans and dark chocolate piled over butter pecan ice cream, and all of it dripping with caramel sauce.

6 ounces pecan halves

6 ounces caramels, unwrapped

1/2 cup heavy cream

1 1/2 quarts high-quality butter pecan ice cream

9 ounces bittersweet chocolate, coarsely chopped

1. Preheat the oven to 325°F.

2. Spread the pecans on a baking sheet and bake until toasted, about 10 minutes. Cool, coarsely chop, and set aside.

3. Put the caramels in a small saucepan over medium heat. When they begin to melt, add the cream and cook, stirring constantly with a wooden spoon, until completely smooth.

4. Place 2 scoops of ice cream in each of 6 dessert bowls. Top each bowl with 2 tablespoons of toasted pecans, 3 tablespoons of chopped chocolate, and a thick layer of warm caramel sauce.

Serves 6

⟶ The caramel sauce can be made ahead and reheated in a microwave or double boiler.

Emergency Grilled Pound Cake Extravaganza

It happens to everybody at some point—an impromptu party takes hold and it's up to the host, pronto. We suggest a field trip to a grocery store with a good bakery. Forage for pound cake that can be toasted on the grill and then lavished with pickups: good chocolate sauce, whipped cream, and fresh berries. Don't ask; don't tell.

Six 1¼-inch slices pound cake (about 10 ounces total)

1½ ounces (3 tablespoons) dark rum

2 tablespoons unsalted butter, softened

Vegetable oil for the grill

1 cup hot fudge or chocolate sauce, warmed

Whipped cream for serving

Fresh raspberries for garnish

1. Prepare a medium fire in a charcoal grill, or preheat a gas or electric grill to medium.

2. Sprinkle both sides of the pound cake with the rum, and then butter both sides. Brush the grill grate with vegetable oil. Grill the slices until golden, about 2 minutes per side.

3. Serve warm, topped with hot fudge sauce, whipped cream, and raspberries.

Serves 6

Screamin' Berry Ice Cream Sandwiches

It would be a crime to let your own private barbecue season expire without at least one great ice cream sandwich. We like to score big snickerdoodle cookies at a bakery because their buttery, cinnamon-intensive profile is a soulful counterpoint to vanilla ice cream folded with fresh berries. That said, play the field with your choice of cookie, ice cream, or berry—the more outrageous the combo, the better.

1 cup fresh berries, plus extra berries for garnish

1 pint high-quality vanilla ice cream, softened

16 large snickerdoodle cookies, frozen for at least 6 hours

1. If using strawberries, hull and cut in half. In a large bowl, fold the berries into the softened ice cream. Transfer to a container, cover, and freeze for at least 1 hour.

2. Remove the ice cream from the freezer and let soften slightly, about 10 minutes. Line a baking sheet with parchment or wax paper. Place 8 frozen cookies, upside down, on the baking sheet. Top each with 1/4 cup of ice cream, spreading the ice cream nearly to the edge of the cookie. Top with the remaining frozen cookies, bottom side down, gently pressing the halves together. Freeze the sandwiches for at least 1 hour. Serve on a platter, garnished with fresh berries.

Makes 8 ice cream sandwiches

Acknowledgments

The recipe for *Patio Daddy-O at the Grill* was one part creative juices, one part eating and testing mania, and one part sharp editorial instincts. We are indebted to the following for sharing their time, culinary secrets, and support:

Our dream editor, Bill LeBlond, the guy who is always there when everything breaks down.

Project editor Amy Treadwell and copy editors Deborah Kops and Rebecca Pepper, three of the best pros in the business.

Reed Darmon, our longtime designer extraordinaire.

Ethel Fleishman, forever our trusted proofreader, sounding board, and arbiter of good taste.

Lena Lencek, Michael Freeman, Mary and Brad Harmon, Roger Porter, Greg Volturo, and Mittie Hellmich, our esteemed friends who shared their treasured recipes, photographs, and cooking paraphernalia.

Index

Table of Equivalents

The exact equivalents in the following tables have been rounded for convenience.

Liquid / Dry Measurements

U.S.	Metric
1/4 teaspoon	1.25 milliliters
1/2 teaspoon	2.5 milliliters
1 teaspoon	5 milliliters
1 tablespoon (3 teaspoons)	15 milliliters
1 fluid ounce (2 tablespoons)	30 milliliters
1/4 cup	60 milliliters
1/3 cup	80 milliliters
1/2 cup	120 milliliters
1 cup	240 milliliters
1 pint (2 cups)	480 milliliters
1 quart (4 cups, 32 ounces)	960 milliliters
1 gallon (4 quarts)	3.84 liters
1 ounce (by weight)	28 grams
1 pound	448 grams
2.2 pounds	1 kilogram

Lengths

U.S.	Metric
1/8 inch	3 millimeters
1/4 inch	6 millimeters
1/2 inch	12 millimeters
1 inch	2.5 centimeters

Liquid Measurements

Bar spoon =	1/2 ounce
1 teaspoon =	1/6 ounce
1 tablespoon =	1/2 ounce
2 tablespoons (pony) =	1 ounce
3 tablespoons (jigger) =	1 1/2 ounces
1/4 cup =	2 ounces
1/3 cup =	3 ounces
1/2 cup =	4 ounces
2/3 cup =	5 ounces
3/4 cup =	6 ounces
1 cup =	8 ounces
1 pint =	16 ounces
1 quart =	32 ounces
750 ml bottle =	25.4 ounces
1 liter bottle =	33.8 ounces
1 medium lemon =	3 tablespoons juice
1 medium lime =	2 tablespoons juice
1 medium orange =	1/3 cup juice

Oven Temperatures

Fahrenheit	Celsius	Gas
250	120	1/2
275	140	1
300	150	2
325	160	3
350	180	4
375	190	5
400	200	6
425	220	7
450	230	8
475	240	9
500	260	10